SHALL I BE A POET INSTEAD?

Shall I Be a Poet Instead?

Lianne M. Bernardo

Copyright © 2017 by Lianne M. Bernardo

All rights reserved. This book or any portion thereof may not be reproduced or used in any manner whatsoever without the express written permission of the publisher except for the use of brief quotations in a book review or scholarly journal.

First Printing: 2017

ISBN: 978-1-7750431-0-2

Note about the font: The font featured in the titles on both the book cover and at the start of each poem is based on my own penmanship (when writing in print).

Hear me, O Muse,
for I suddenly recall myself:
long have I been silent,
writing hand stayed,
but no more.

Lend me your courage
as I unleash my words
into the night.

WORDS (Part 1)

How does one
prompt the words to come out?
They are lost inside,
the tumults of an ever-thinking mind:
unformed, disjointed, searching,
threatening to shrivel up.

How does one
write the truest of words on paper?

SHALL I BE A POET INSTEAD?

Shall I be a poet instead?
For it is the only way to express, it seems,
what is bottled up in
the storage boxes of my mind,
the refracted visages of my heart.
To write down the words
lest they crumble into dust;
to capture the fleeting moments
before they drift away, gone forever.
With these words I pin my dreams,
those lofty clouds that sail
across boundless skies day in, day out
before my very eyes.
Shall I be a poet instead?

STARTING OVER

Somewhere there is a man
taking his last drink.
Somewhere there is a woman
dragging on her last cigarette.

Out there in the world
there is a person
breaking their last promise
whilst elsewhere there is another
taking their first step.

Life is starting over.

Doom

Doomed are the lovers
fated to die;
they all fall down,
their legs of stone.

BADLANDS

The plains lie barren, silent in its efforts;
only the sun and heat remains.
The void hides the unmarked graves
of travellers gone astray without a compass;
the silence masks the sounds of
bone grinding against bone.

But wait! Hold your breath,
press your ear against the wind:
above the cloying hum of silence
is the rattling of torn skeletons.

THE FIRST ELEGY TO A.R--

Just like that, three little words
and cold reality settles in—
A bright light has flickered out
from this thing called life,
leaving the world greyer, with less song.
Words are worthless here
to measure the weight of this loss,
this void left in her wake.
There will be much anguish
in the days to come;
no amount of tears can
fully express the heartbreak,
the desolation that lies ahead.

But beneath the colossal shadow of grief
lies some secret knowledge:
like your namesake's thread bringing
the hero out of the monster's maze,
you have followed your own thread
back into the arms of the Lord.

MUSEUM

Welcome to my museum
of never-will-be's,
hallmarks of missed opportunities,
and shattered dreams.
Read my testimony here
of chances that slipped by,
of unforeseen moments lost
to the neuroses and the uncertainty.
The consciousness wills onward
but the mind's eye lingers
upon the walls of this brimming exhibition.

POTHOLES

The road I travel on is riddled with potholes
covered in black mortar to hide their murky depths.
Unwittingly I plough through them and fall,
the jolt disorienting me out of myself.

The road ahead of me is unforeseen,
the destination is vague at best.
I navigate around the hollows
like that of an old woman:
every now and then I fall anyway.

LIFE SUPPORT (Part 1)

Emptiness.

Today my world is a barren wasteland,
the air devoid of sweetness
and old dreams lie on life support—
one beat, two beats.

My head is confused,
my gut is stunned,
and my heart is oddly silent.

Won't someone help me out?

LIFE SUPPORT (Part II)

It should be cheerless skies
to match the emptiness felt.
Instead it is shining bright,
the sun burning into my soul,
discomfort transforming
into a personal hell.

Perhaps it is time to take
  the dreams off life support,
  bury the feelings in an unmarked grave
  with no cenotaph to commemorate;
  turn back the clock and resume waking life
  without expectation, without anticipation,
  return the heart to lockdown mode.

But nothing refuses to fit back in,
the old storage bins now outgrown
and winter is still well away.
Is it fruitless to hope?
I ask myself again
  and again
  and again.

MY LIFE

I measure my life
   by the things I've done,
   the obstacles I've faced,
   climbed, and overcome.

I measure my life
   by the mistakes I've made,
   the opportunities I've missed,
   my regrets.

I measure my life
   by the weight of the stars—
   In short, I hazard a guess;
   it's somewhere along those lines.

GOLD MOON

Gold moon,
lend me your magic,
your elusive charm.
You hover over the inky horizon
luminous, larger than life
with your three-fourths grin.

Gold moon,
lend me your cape;
illuminate me with your shine,
watch me take flight.

BROKEN GROUND

Treading carefully over
detonated dreams,
shattered preconceptions,
shredded expectations.
My feet are covered in blisters,
bleeding from the remnants—

—What there is left to give up?

(Much, it seems.)

WORDS (Part II)

My heart is made of words
spun tightly around and around
layer upon layer
until they form a mass,
an illegible chain of appellation.
Only to whom I give it to
will read them inch by inch,
volume upon volume,
every secret word I've strung.

YEARNING

A behemoth of silence
stretches out before my shadow,
craving to swallow up the empty spaces.

Endless horizons
lies beyond the field of vision
and with it stands restless feet that beg to walk.

WHERE HAVE THE DREAMERS GONE?

Where have the dreamers gone
and where have they taken their dreams?
Replaced are golems that speak
of matters that are merely transient.
They will fade into obscurity,
leaving not even a shadow in their wake.

SLEEPING GIANTS

My reluctant miracles convalesce
until they become sleeping giants,
the stuff of legends.

GLASS SKY

This glass sky that I cannot touch
surely cannot be real
with its swirls of white and pink
and grey against eternal blue,
a confectionery of colour and light.

Surely this ephemeral dome is
a reflection of the sea,
the blue-grey waves that never sleep
always drifting,
onward and upward.

And where do they meet,
the glass sky and the sleepless waters?
With a breath, a tear, a salty kiss.

SHY HEART

I compose imaginary letters to my almost loves,
those who seized my heart but nothing happened,
to those I failed to act upon, shy heart at work.

AUTUMN (Part I)

Autumn is for the unrequited love:
like the waning summer days
their hope lingers on
even as the leaves shift colour, fade, and fall
leaving branches bare, exposed
to the coming frost.

AUTUMN (Part II)

Autumn is for the hopeful:
like the changing winds it is
a season of maturity;
of realisations and revelations,
the sober reality after the restless summer days,
cooler weather with cooler tempers
and precious hopes blooming against
the coming of twilight.

GREETINGS, NIGHT

Look up to the night sky,
that sea of velvet darkness,
and say hello to the stars
revealing themselves against the half-moon
in full force.

LOSING HOPE

Is this what giving up feels like?
The hollowness where the heartbeats were,
the eerie calm replacing the fury
of emotions, of thoughts,
the tumultuousness deep in the gut.

Is this what giving up feels like
when you find yourself at a loss of words,
not from the depth of feeling
but from an absence of passion?

A HAUNTING

A kiss on the lips that lingers
despite the absence of touch.
An embrace from a shadow
that does not exist.
A deep longing for something
never felt, never known
and yet haunts every step,
sensed with every turn--
a haunting without a ghost.

BLANK PAGE

Hours slide by
—tick, tick, tick—
and an empty canvas remains,
a white page left blank,
and a mind weighing heavily
with light-speed
    everything,
    and nothing,
    and anything in between.

LOVE

When I love, it will be forever;
I will immortalise you with my words,
painting out all the things I do not say out loud.

When I love, it will be endless;
I will not shy from embracing you often,
keep you close as you are alive in my heart.

ORIGIN STORIES

Let us share origin stories,
of where our journeys began.
For some began at conception,
the long passage to self-actualisation.
For others it began later on in life,
a start and stop in the middle of the road.
Paths change, landslides and dead ends emerge,
prompting sudden endings and new beginnings,
life ever-evolving.

RECOVERY

Scalding heart recovering from burns
left by the careless lover (the nerve of the man).
Ice cannot soothe or heal the wounds,
only open air and time.

FEAR

When the words run out
where will that leave me?
All the thoughts circling
in my head
but my tongue an empty
shriveled vessel,
the pen in my hand still.

IN THE DARK

Blinded, we stumble into the abyss
feeble, uncertain, grasping for purchase—
but we threw away all the rocks
and covered up the foot holes with grout.
In the dark we've forgotten all the lessons,
all the experiences on how to proceed,
and the lamp used to brighten the way
we left at home, broken and in disarray.
Where does that leave us?
Alone, divided, paralysed, in the dark.

ASSEMBLY BLOCKS

If only I can piece together the future
with discarded crumbs from the present
and relics from a past long gone.

If only it were that simple.

FEELINGS

Take this furor away from me,
this chest of feelings:
whether it be the downpour of grief
or the heavy fog of doubt,
the rumbling fireball of irritation,
or the sudden wave of that thing called love.
They grip me, nail me down,
seize me like a vise—
The intensity of their comings and goings
are a safety hazard.

WAITING

Waiting,
it's all about the waiting:
the pause between
one breath and two breath;
the space between words,
the silence before the fall.

FIRING LINE

It's trial by fire;
they don't care
if you crash and burn
whilst they rise above the fumes.

WORDS (Part III)

Reduce my sentences to something leaner,
more digestible for consumption.
With it the flavour is lost:
the texture, the characteristics
that make it what it is.

Put down the instrument;
you do not know
how to wield it.

HIDDEN LIGHT

Light and darkness
and the breaking of dawn;
and somewhere in the deep waters,
an independent source of light.

RUST

Somewhere in the deep dark wood
lies a pool whose depth is unknown
but sits hidden amongst the poplars.
The naked eye cannot see it
but its colour is crimson,
its scent is that of rust—
it threatens to consume.

ASPIRATIONS

Outstretched trees
attempting to touch the sky,
something beyond the fissures,
their broken trunks
still rooted in the earth.

WINTER DOME

The north sky
punctures through the ice dome
of the winter world
glittering like a million crystals,
sloughing over weather-weary trees.

PORTRAITS

The portraits—
they tell a story
of lifestyles toiled
and lives lost,
buildings abandoned
to the ruin of time.

THE MARTYR

The blood is absent on the fallen martyr:
it is invisible, consumed by her dark robes
and masked by the roses and lilies
that fall from her chest and spill beyond
her lifeless arms.
The flowers are dead,
they no longer bloom forevermore;
they cascade downward onto the hard earth,
flourishing the cold plains of death instead.

UNCERTAINTY

Darkness is a miasma of the world these days:
the black-banded fellows are marching in
whilst the rest of us watch,
wide-eyed with a bewildered moan.
Anger displaced, heading nowhere
—whatever is to be done?

DOUBT

A vaulting crescendo sky high
—over fields and valleys and
snow-capped mountains—
that end with a plummet so deep,
so dark, that the doubts consume
to a madness that leaves you questioning
everything you see and come to believe:
        thc roundness of the moon,
        the brightness of the star,
        the ferocity of the sun.

AN EPITAPH (OF SORTS)

And when I die
they will stumble across my notebooks
filled with incomplete thoughts,
half-realised dreams,
fractured illusions,
grand attempts at greatness,
proficiency, and productivity.

ABOUT THE AUTHOR

Lianne M. Bernardo is from Canada. She has previously written for high school and university publications, online e-zines, and Youth Speak News at the Catholic Register whilst accumulating a stack of unpublished content ranging from novel-length stories to poetry.

Shall I be a Poet Instead? is her first poetry collection.

www.ingramcontent.com/pod-product-compliance
Ingram Content Group UK Ltd.
Pitfield, Milton Keynes, MK11 3LW, UK
UKHW041837200726
13854UKWH00003BA/1184